Meet the Stars of

by Samantha Calderone

SCHOLASTIC INC.

New York   Toronto   London   Auckland   Sydney
Mexico City   New Delhi   Hong Kong

TABLE OF CONTENTS

Introduction

They say your high school years are the best years of your life. But let's face it, everyone knows that high school isn't all fun and games. It can in fact be downright stressful. Sometimes fitting in socially is more of a challenge — and more of a priority — than acing a biology exam.

Earning a place among the social elite can secure a high school experience full of party invitations, dances, and football games. It means always having a place to sit at the cool lunch table. Conversely, many teens totally lose self-esteem if they don't "fit in" with a certain group. They feel as though they're not popular.

Hmm, popular?

Sounds like a good title for a television show, huh?

When television producers Ryan Murphy and Gina Matthews discussed developing a new drama series for the WB network, they thought of the one thing most people want — to be popular. Ryan says the universal theme of wanting to be accepted, wanting to belong, wanting to be *wanted* is one that extends far beyond the hallways of high school. "Whether you want to be popular in your job, or you want to have that guy say that he loves you back, or you want to have the right kind of friends or be liked by the right kind of people, it never ends," he explains.

That "wanting" starts in high school. Before the show premiered, Ryan explained to a group of journalists that the popularity theme is something tweens and teens can especially relate to. "The reason we created the show was Gina and I were having a conversation one day about our high school experiences. They were very similar. The first two years in high school we were both incredibly unpopular and geeky."

Luckily, Ryan and Gina were able to find the humor in it all and created quirky, over-the-top characters who inhabit the hallways of Kennedy High. High school is full of cliques — the cheerleaders, the jocks, the brains, the geeks. So they created the stereotypical character types that exist in every high school. Ryan explained, "This show is a satire. So we make a point of how superficial people can be."

Popular premiered on Wednesday, September 29, 1999, and has developed into a favorite show among teens and tweens. Millions of viewers tune in each week to see nasty cheerleaders Nicole Julian and Mary Cherry torment popular wanna-bes Sam McPherson and Carmen Ferrera. Beautiful Brooke McQueen seems to have it all — looks, money, and popularity — but yet is often so unhappy. Classmates Lily Esposito, Harrison John, Josh Ford, and Mike "Sugar Daddy" Bernadino, who round out the clan, try not to get caught up in the games their friends play.

There are nine main actors who bring these memorable characters to life and make *Popular* worth watching every week. Each actor has dealt with acceptance and rejection, sometimes in ways similar to how his or her respective character has managed. Their roads to fame were filled with fun, sadness, and inspiring life lessons. Let's take a look at the actors before they were "popular."

LESLIE BIBB
is Brooke McQueen

Everyone assumes it's great at the top. Just ask Brooke McQueen. For practically her entire life she's been, socially anyway, "best of breed." On the surface, Brooke seems an obvious choice. She is arguably the prettiest girl in school, wears expensive designer clothes, and has the ability to get any guy she wants at the snap of her fingers. Brooke is also one of the head Glamazon cheerleaders and Kennedy High's homecoming queen. So what's wrong with this picture?

It would be a mistake to judge Brooke by her outside appearance. Sure, she has the makings of an "it" girl, from her shiny blond highlights to her Prada shoes. But inside, she's confused about everything from the meaning of life to where she fits in the big picture. Her mother left when Brooke was a young girl, leaving the parenting duties to Brooke's father. For a long time Brooke felt responsible for her mother's departure, even though her father had assured her that it wasn't the case. She developed an eating disorder in her early teens and still has food and body issues to this day. She does *not* have it all together. She's just trying to take life one day at a time.

Actress Leslie Bibb says Brooke is the toughest character to play. "She's the one *nobody* should like. I describe Brooke as the 'it' girl, the Gwyneth Paltrow of high school." But Leslie notes that Brooke is really much easier to relate to than people think. "She still has the same insecurities that everyone else does."

Leslie says playing Brooke is a stretch because she and her character really don't have too much in common. "I'm a country girl," Leslie says proudly. "I grew up on a farm, had to feed the horses, weed the garden, mow the lawn." Her farm girl roots are a world away from Brooke's princesslike existence. Still, Leslie told *TV Guide,* she can relate to the pressure her character feels. "I am equally as hard on myself."

Girls, Girls, Girls

Leslie is the youngest of four girls in her family. She was born in Bismarck, North Dakota, and raised in Nelson County, Virginia, a rural area located outside of Richmond. When Leslie was three, her father died, and she and her sisters were raised by her single mother, who often worked several jobs to support the family. Leslie admires her mom and sisters for all that they did to keep the family together. "My mom taught her girls not to be bossed around," the young actress says. "She was really fantastic with us. I always felt I could go to her to talk about anything — money, boyfriends, friends. We're very open in our family."

With a house full of women, Leslie quickly learned to voice her opinion and stand up for herself, especially when it came to borrowing one another's clothes. Her sisters were more like Brooke McQueen than she ever was. "Tricia," Leslie says, "was the 'it' girl. And my sister Kim was the head cheerleader and had a beautiful boyfriend." Leslie gushes dreamily when she talks about how much she loves them. "I wanted to be like them."

There were also times she wanted to kill them. Not really, of course. But, as Leslie explains, "They tortured me when I was little. One time they bound me and muzzled me and threw me in my mother's shower!" Leslie laughs hysterically when she recalls her sisters' antics. "They were supposed to be watching me while my mom was downstairs with her bridge club."

Pulling pranks on one another was just a playful way for the girls to express how much they loved one another. Because Leslie was the youngest, she was often the victim of taunting and teasing. But she took it in stride because she knew that her sisters were only having fun. When Leslie's older sisters settled down and started families of their own, they still remained very connected to one another and often called on Leslie to baby-sit. "I still think they are the coolest," she asserts.

During junior high and high school, Leslie was an excellent student, a terrific athlete (she played tennis), a cheerleader, and a volunteer tutor for inner-city second graders. When Leslie was a teenager, she and her mom moved to Richmond, Virginia. Leslie was bummed to leave the farm but excited about going to a new high school. She'd loved her old high school. Each of her sisters had gone there. But, Leslie says, there were times when she felt she was being compared to her sisters in a way that tended to stifle her individuality. At her new school, St. Gertrude's High, Leslie was able to stand out on her own.

Model Student

It didn't take long for the gang at St. Gertrude's, a girls' Catholic high school, to get to know Leslie. For starters, the school was much smaller than Leslie's other school — there were only thirty-eight girls in her grade. Modestly, Leslie will say that she wasn't popular or that she wasn't particularly attractive when she was younger. Not true. In fact, Leslie was the kind of girl who could get along with anyone. She had an earnest, caring nature that was downright infectious. And she was beautiful, just not in a glamorous, look-at-me kind of way, but rather in a down-to-earth, girl-next-door kind of way.

One day her sister Tricia caught an episode of Oprah Winfrey's talk show and immediately thought of Leslie. Oprah's show was conducting a nationwide teen model search. The winner would land a modeling contract. Tricia thought her baby sister was a perfect candidate, so she hastily scribbled down the address. She frantically called her mother and begged her to send in some pictures of Leslie. Leslie's mom took two fresh pictures with the family camera and sent them into the talk show.

Leslie didn't expect to win. She didn't even think anyone would see her pictures. She knew that a contest like this would attract thousands of people and that her chances of making it were very slim.

She was really surprised then when she got a call several weeks later from a woman at *The Oprah Winfrey Show* informing her that she was one of sixty-three finalists in the teen model search contest. Oprah wanted to fly each of the girls to Chicago, where the show is taped, for a final selection process. Leslie practically hung up on the woman because she was sure this was a hoax. She figured one of her sisters was playing a prank on her as they had many times before. But no, the woman assured her, this was for real.

Only sixteen at the time, Leslie was stoked about going to Chicago and being on television. It was so exciting and surreal. She and her mother quickly made plans to go. All of the contestants flew into Chicago for the big day and stayed at a swanky downtown hotel. Then, through a preliminary judging process, the field was narrowed to twenty girls. Among them was Leslie. The day of the show, the finalists were driven to Oprah's studio, where they met supermodel judges Iman, Linda Evangelista, and modeling agency executive John Casablancas. Leslie was nervous. But her mother assured her that no matter what, this was going to be an experience she'd never forget, and advised her to be grateful for the opportunity.

The entire show was devoted to the contest. In the end, Oprah announced that Leslie Bibb had *won*. She would receive a modeling contract with Elite Model Management and have the opportunity to travel and work with some of the most prestigious people in the business. Leslie froze in disbelief. One by one, the other contestants walked over to Leslie and congratulated her. Then it hit her, Leslie says. "I completely spazzed out!"

First, Leslie and her mother returned to Richmond so Leslie could finish out the school year. Then the freshly minted model was off to Japan for a series of jobs. "It was such an exciting thing. It was like winning the lottery," Leslie says of the contest. "The summer before I was baby-sitting for my sisters' kids. Then the next summer I was modeling in Japan."

While things seemed picture-perfect for Leslie, she says that it wasn't the case when she returned to St. Gertrude's. "I was a girl who mothers thought was pretty, but not to the other girls in school. When I won, I remember these girls going, 'You won? Why?' I was so not thought of as pretty in my school. My classmates were stunned when I won."

College or Show Business?

After Leslie graduated from St. Gertrude's she enrolled in the University of Virginia with hopes of becoming a lawyer someday. But in the back of her mind, she kind of wondered "what if?" What if she continued modeling? That *could* lead to acting, something she'd always wanted to do. After a lot of soul-searching, Leslie decided that if she was going to make a serious go of an acting career, she would need to put forth a hundred percent effort. She put college on hold and moved to New York City. She continued modeling to pay the bills, but between modeling jobs, she took acting classes at the William Esper acting studios. After several years, Leslie felt ready to try her luck in TV and movies. She packed her bags for Los Angeles.

Soon after landing in LA, Leslie found an agent who booked her in her first film, Howard Stern's *Private Parts*. Leslie had a small role in the movie as an NBC tour guide. So what was it like working with the controversial radio star? Leslie says the shock jock couldn't have been cooler. "Howard was incredibly nice to me on the set of *Private Parts*," Leslie told the *Calgary Sun* newspaper, adding that these days "he's a big fan of *Popular*."

Like many actors and actresses who are just starting out, Leslie landed a smorgasbord of guest-starring roles on television shows. She appeared on *Home Improvement*, *Just Shoot Me*, *Fired Up*, and

Early Edition. For the independent film *The Young Unknowns,* Leslie dyed her natural brown hair a bold, brassy shade of blond. Before the color had faded, she landed an audition for *Popular.* Brooke McQueen was envisioned as the stereotypical blond cheerleader, so Leslie was extra glad she hadn't dyed her hair back.

She had the hair thing right — unfortunately, she wasn't feeling very well the day of the audition. She had the flu! She really wanted to move the tryout to another day, but her manager urged her not to miss this opportunity. So, Leslie says, she went to the audition with a scratchy throat and practically no energy. Still, she not only managed to get through the reading, she nailed the part! She's been a blond ever since. Leslie's good fortune continued that same week when she also found out she'd landed a lead role in the teen thriller *The Skulls* opposite *Dawson's Creek* star Joshua Jackson. Talk about hitting the lottery!

Giving Back

Although she's been super lucky in a tough, competitive, and glamorous career, Leslie hasn't forgotten where she came from. Her mother instilled an admirable work ethic in all her daughters, as well as the philosophy that when you have, you should always give back. Leslie gives back every Sunday to an organization called The Unusual Suspects, which is located in LA's juvenile hall.

Leslie and several other actors and actresses help the teens there write and act out plays. Leslie says she's fulfilled by her weekly visits because the kids in the program really try. "I almost feel guilty about how much I get out of these Sundays," Leslie confessed to *Teen Movieline*. "I go in feeling empty from work, and when I leave I feel full again. It's the best two hours of my week."

CARLY POPE
is Sam McPherson

Sam McPherson is probably one of the most typical teenagers around. At sixteen, life is more confusing for her than it ever has been — in and out of school. Her home life took a turn for the weird. Sam *thought* she and her mom were doing just fine together after her father's death. Then her mom went on a solo vacation, met up with Brooke McQueen's father — and fell in love. *Then* they decided to move in together. Which meant Sam and Brooke had to live under the same roof, share the same bathroom, and use the same phone. Given that Brooke McQueen has long been Sam's archrival, this was not a good thing.

At school, Sam feels like one of the people always trying to fit in. She's a good student, but she's not a geek. She gets along with most everyone, but she's not "popular." One of her best friends, Harrison John, is in love with Brooke, which annoys Sam. And then there's her own relationship with Brooke: The one person she can't stand is now the one person she can't get away from. Deep down inside, Sam realizes there is a hint of jealousy in her own feelings. Brooke has everything Sam secretly wants — looks, great clothes, guys gawking at her, and popularity.

Actress Carly Pope says she can totally relate to her character's issues and dilemmas. "We have a broad similarity, the confusion that goes on at sixteen," Carly says. "I think it's more of an internal confusion, trying to figure things out. And I can relate to that." Carly told *Teen* magazine that the show is a classic look at how everybody just wants to fit in. "It's really important for people to realize that everybody's going to experience the same emotions, the same ups and downs."

Carly makes it sound so simple. But when a person goes through soul-searching times, it helps to have someone to talk to. For Carly, getting through high school was a lot easier thanks to her older brother, Kris. She told *Teen,* "Kris was in his last year of high school when I was in my first. It was nice to realize that he was going through similar experiences but knew exactly how to deal with them for both of us."

"Jill" of All Trades

Carly was born and raised in Vancouver, British Columbia, Canada. Vancouver is located in the westernmost region of Canada, directly north of Washington State, and about a three-hour flight from Los Angeles. Because her two siblings are boys (Kris is older, Alex is younger), Carly grew up a bit of a tomboy. Early on, the naturally athletic Carly could run, throw a ball, and hit, swim, and snowboard just as well as any of the boys in her town. But Carly wasn't just a jockette. She was an all-star in the classroom, too. During her elementary school years Carly attended a school where all of her classes were taught in French. Needless to say, Carly became proficient in the language and is still bilingual.

When it came time to go to high school, Carly enrolled in Vancouver's Lord Byng High School, where all of the classes were taught in English. As a teenager, Carly was heavily involved with school athletics and remained an excellent student. Plus, she was popular.

Carly's not one to ramble on about her high school experience. But when asked, she does admit that she had a lot of friends in high school and that overall her high school years were memorable in a good way. She told *YM* magazine that her school really wasn't at all like *Popular*'s Kennedy High, especially during her senior year. That's when the social cliques decided to disband. "The class realized that we'd been shutting each other out for too long. It taught me that you can form the deepest friendship with someone you might have [previously] disregarded because you thought you had to stay in your tiny group."

One group Carly decided she wanted to

get to know better was the kids in the high school drama department. She joined the theater club and soon realized how much fun it was to transform herself into different characters. A big reader, Carly used to devour books and use her vivid imagination to bring the stories to life. Theater was a good fit for Carly because she had an incredible knack for understanding and applying the material in a believable way.

Little by little, Carly's efforts were rewarded, and she started to branch out by doing some local work in film and television. Her first "big" role was actually a small one in the feature film *Disturbing Behavior*, which starred hottie James Marsden and featured fellow Canadian Brendan Fehr (*Roswell*). She followed that up with a part in the ABC television movie *Our Guys: Outrage in Glen Ridge*, where she and Brendan met up once again. Carly later had roles in the children's film *Aliens in the Wild, Wild West* and the Showtime cable movie *A Cooler Climate*. She appeared in the movie *Snow Day* and an

NBC movie of the week titled *I've Been Waiting for You.* Her career was off to an incredible start, to say the least.

But because education was so important to her, Carly enrolled in a local university after graduating from Lord Byng in 1998. Her days as a coed, however, were numbered when Carly's agent called her to audition for the role of Brooke McQueen in *Popular.* Yes, that's right, Carly *originally* read for the Brooke role. But when the producers saw her, they immediately knew they had found their Sam McPherson.

Carly told *Cosmo Girl* magazine that she knew from the get-go she was reading for the wrong role when she did Brooke's lines. "I realized I didn't really believe myself in that role," Carly said. "The execs must have noticed it, too, because they asked if I'd read for the part of Sam instead."

Suzanne Daniels, president of entertainment at the WB network, recalled Carly's audition to *TV Guide.* "About thirty seconds after she opened her mouth, we knew she had the role." Suzanne said she was perfect for Sam because "she's not the blond cheerleader type."

Star Trip

Carly and the *Popular* gang filmed the pilot (first episode) in early 1999. The WB network snatched it up in no time. In addition to landing a regular series gig, Carly got word that she was cast in a lead role for the ABC television movie *Trapped in a Purple Haze*. That meant she'd have to put college on the back burner, a decision that Carly at times feels conflicted about. After all, she was just beginning to see what college life was all about, and all of a sudden she had to stop and move to Los Angeles, away from her family and close friends. It was quite a culture shock moving from peaceful Vancouver to the frenetic freeways and instant fame of Hollywood.

Carly's friend Brendan Fehr was going through a very similar situation. He, too, had landed a lead role, on the WB series *Roswell*. And moving to Los Angeles from

Canada was quite a change of pace for the young actor. The two friends spent a lot of time together, talking about all of the exciting things that were happening to them. At times they were scared and a little confused about the hoopla that goes with the territory of being an actor. Carly told *YM* magazine, "I feel a little like the new kid in school, trying to figure out where I fit in." While Carly might at times feel conflicted about her place in Hollywood, one thing is certain. Hollywood has made room for her and Brendan. As their respective shows ended their first season, Carly and Brendan found themselves among a prestigious group as two of *Teen People*'s "The Hottest 25 Under 25."

To keep things in check, Carly flies home to visit her family as often as possible. She considers herself a private person and admits that being famous is a concept she still can't comprehend. "I don't understand what fame or celebrity means," Carly says with exasperation. "I wish somebody could explain to me that it's okay or that it's logical, because to me it's not. . . . I get very awkward and uncomfortable in public situations."

Of course Carly is appreciative when people come up to her and remark how much they like the show. Like it or not, *she* is popular. "It's very flattering and I love that people respond to the character. I think that's so amazing that I can evoke a response in people that's a positive one."

BRYCE JOHNSON
is Josh Ford

Every school has a Josh Ford, a dream-boat of a guy who's good-looking, athletic, a decent student, *and* has a winning per-sonality. The Josh Ford types often date the most popular girls in school. In other words, the Brooke McQueen types. In *Popular,* Josh isn't quite that stereotypical, though he does possess some "jock" traits. He's kind to his friends and doesn't make fun of people who are different. Unlike some popular boys, Josh doesn't do things to please other people. He does things that fulfill him. For example, Josh is one of Kennedy High's best football players. Be-cause of his talent, not only did the team have a shot at the championships, Josh had a chance at a college football scholar-ship. But one day as Josh was walking down the hall to class, he saw a sign for open auditions for the school musical production of *South Pacific*. It was as if a light went off in his head. Singing was something he always secretly enjoyed but was often too shy to do in front of his friends. Josh teetered on whether to try out. He knew it would interfere with his commitment to the football team. But right in the middle of football practice, Josh decided to go for it. He realized he didn't want to look back later in life and wonder what might have been. Still in his uniform, he ran as fast as he could across the field, into the school, and right onto the stage for his audition. His instincts proved right — he landed the lead role! While he was elated about his new accomplishment, his girlfriend, Brooke, thought his newfound passion was a bit geeky. Her lack of support caused tension in their relationship, and for a while the two split.

Josh managed to cope, although it was difficult. After all, who doesn't want to be liked and respected by his or her peers? It was pressure that Josh really didn't want or need. But he handled it well, and despite his father's protests, he followed his heart to the stage and wowed the crowd.

That kind of determination and commitment is exactly what lies inside of actor Bryce Johnson. Bryce, after all, was a former high school jock turned actor himself. Playing Josh, says Bryce, is definitely something he can relate to. "A lot of the characteristics that I had in high school, that's what I put into the character," he explains. "We have a lot of the same personality traits. We both love sports, we respect women, we're just overall pretty good guys. We're in a lot of the same situations, and it's kind of neat to get to play those out again and relive those moments. He's not a jerk. He's not out to hurt anybody. I think that's a really important quality, and I love the fact that he's like that. It's cool. I like to be a good role model, and I like younger viewers to look up to a role like that."

"I Decided to Go for It"

Bryce was always a popular kid. Born in Reno, Nevada, and raised in Denver, Colorado, and later, Sioux City, Iowa, Bryce quickly learned how to adapt to new social situations. He's the middle of three boys in his family and was always into competitions. Bryce delved into extracurricular activities with relish. He loved playing soccer, golf, baseball, and basketball and served as a member of his school's student council. He was a well-rounded guy — except for when it came to grades. "I wasn't really studious just because," Bryce says with a shrug. "I could have gotten good grades if I really applied myself. But I was an average student and that was okay for me."

Bryce enjoyed hanging out with his friends, playing sports, and dating. But when it came to planning his future, he felt that college might not be right for him. It wasn't that he was opposed to school. He just possessed a keen curiosity for acting. He daydreamed about what it would be like to live in Los Angeles and be an actor. And even though he'd never done any acting before, he just *knew* it was for him. So during his junior year of high school, he concluded that his future was going to be in show business. "I decided to go for it," Bryce says of his chosen path.

Upon graduating from high school, Bryce wanted to learn as much as possible about his chosen path. While going to a four-year college wasn't in his original game plan, enrolling in Western Iowa Tech Community College to take some acting classes was a good alternative. He knew he'd have to buckle down if he really wanted to make it as an actor, so he saved as much money as he could by working at the local Southern Hills Mall. In the meantime, Bryce learned about a performing arts school in Pasadena, California, called the American Academy of Dramatic Arts. He went ahead and applied. It's a school that focuses on training actors. "Once I got accepted, that kind of got the ball rolling," Bryce says.

At age nineteen, Bryce packed his personal belongings into his Ford Taurus and drove west, determined to make it. Once in Los Angeles, he worked hard trying to learn the ropes of the business. Between acting classes and workshops he waited tables and did telemarketing jobs. During the summer of 1998, his persistence paid off. He landed a role in *Saving Grace,* a television pilot. The show didn't get picked up by any networks, but as is often the case, one acting job leads to another. Bryce then nabbed a five-day stint on MTV's *Undressed.* He told the *Sioux City Journal,* "We shot five episodes in five days. I worked eighty hours. That was a vicious week."

Once the MTV job was over, Bryce was back to square one — at that moment, he didn't have another acting job lined up. He thought he'd have to go back to being a waiter, but then his agent called about auditioning for *Popular.* Next thing he knew, Bryce found himself cast as the lead cutie on one of the most talked-about shows of the 1999–2000 television season, for which he's totally stoked. "I go to work five

days a week doing something I love,"
Bryce told the *Sioux City Journal*.

Hottie With a Cause

Although Bryce was euphoric over his
career taking off, he was bummed that he
couldn't share it much with his friends and
family back home in Iowa. The Sioux City
cable system didn't carry the WB network,
so no one he knew could watch *Popular*.
The WB is still a relatively young network
and doesn't air everywhere, like NBC and
ABC do. Even Bryce's mom, who was so
proud of her son's accomplishments,
couldn't watch him every week on television. Of course Bryce could send his mom
tapes of the show every week, but what
about the other thousands upon thousands
of people the Sioux City cable system
serves? What if *they* wanted to see *Popular* or other WB shows like *Felicity, Dawson's Creek,* or *Buffy* and couldn't because
they weren't offered the choice?

Along with some executives and other stars of the WB, Bryce decided to try to remedy this situation. In October 1999, shortly after *Popular* premiered, WB CEO Jamie Kellner, Bryce, and fellow WB star Shannen Doherty (*Charmed*) flew to Sioux City for a rally in hopes of encouraging the CableONE network to add the WB to its lineup.

The trip also included a personal appearance at the Southern Hills Mall, where Bryce once worked. The celebrated return home was exciting and surreal for Bryce. "It was like something you ask for in a diary. My dreams had come true," Bryce gushed to the *Sioux City Journal*. "When you leave a place to start a career, you have no idea that you're going to fly back three years later with the head of a network and Shannen Doherty."

Sadly, the rally proved unsuccessful, and as we went to press, the town was still without a WB station. But Bryce felt this experience was invaluable. "What I like about acting is just being able to work in front of an audience of millions and millions of viewers and get paid to do it." Any downsides? "I don't get to do it enough," Bryce says. Otherwise, "there's not a bad thing about it that I've discovered yet."

SARA RUE
is Carmen Ferrera

Looking in from the outside is how Carmen Ferrera feels when she enters Kennedy High School each morning. That does *not* feel good. It's often difficult for Carmen to go to school each day when she feels she doesn't measure up to her classmates — especially Brooke McQueen, Nicole Julian, and Mary Cherry. All three have what Carmen has longed for her entire life — good looks, boyfriends, money, and most of all, popularity.

While Carmen can count on best friends Sam McPherson, Harrison John, and Lily Esposito, still she wants more. She, more than her circle of close friends, feels the need to belong to the popular crowd. For some reason, their approval of her, their acceptance of her is extremely important to her. So important that at times she sacrifices being true to herself. In the show's first season, all she wanted was a chance to be a cheerleader. Joining the Glamazons would be the ultimate symbol of acceptance for Carmen. But the first go-around with nasty head cheerleader Nicole Julian went sour. Even though Carmen was talented enough to make the squad, Nicole let her know that she wouldn't make the cut because she was too heavy.

That brutal judgment would be enough to sink any high school girl's dreams, but Carmen hung in and eventually proved that she belonged on the squad, much to Nicole's chagrin. That kind of spirit and determination, says actress Sara Rue, is what she likes most about playing Carmen. "I think if my high school life had been as rocky as Carmen's I would not have dealt as well as she does. She just picks up, dusts herself off, and starts all over again. I'm constantly impressed by her."

A lot of what acting is about is relating to one's character, and Sara says that while her high school life wasn't like Carmen's, she *has* experienced similar frustrating situations. Sara has never been thin — a fact she's proud of. "I've never been skinny," she told Tacoma's *News Tribune.* "I've never been model thin. Weight hasn't been an issue. It's not my battle in life."

What *has* been a challenge for Sara is the same challenge faced by all actors — proving that she deserves a shot to be seen. And after more than twelve years as a professional actress, she's shown, with the same brand of Carmen Ferrera determination that she's good and that looks shouldn't matter. The entertainment industry is jammed with thin, shapely girls. Sara says her "plus" size has been a plus for her. "Real thin girls are looked at as being the pretty girls, and no matter how hard they study or how well they do, they're always the pretty girls," Sara explained to reporters at a WB press conference last summer. "It's nice to be acknowledged for your work instead of your body."

A Star Is Born

It would be hard not to acknowledge Sara for her work. She's one of the most talented and hardest-working actresses on television. It's also "the family business." Sara's father was a Broadway stage manager, and her mom was a working stage actress. From the time Sara uttered her first cries in her parents' Manhattan apartment, it was clear she had a dramatic flair. "I can't remember wanting to be anything else," Sara says matter-of-factly.

New York is one of the richest cultural centers in the world, and young Sara absorbed every bit of it. Most people only dream of having the kind of life that Sara had during her childhood. Thanks to her parents' creative ventures, she was exposed to some of the most talented theater actors and singers in the world. They inspired her. All she could think was "I can do this." She traveled with her parents all over the country, even one time to Alaska where her mother was performing in a play. The life of an actress, Sara soon learned, was hard work but certainly fascinating.

Mesmerized by the magic of theater, the magic of creating characters and telling stories, young Sara soon pleaded with her parents to let her give acting a try. Initially, Sara thought, becoming an actress would be a no-brainer. After all, she practically grew up backstage while watching professional actors do their stuff. But her parents tried to discourage her from following in their footsteps. Sara explains, "They knew it was a really hard business, and they didn't want me to get into it." But Sara convinced them that this was really what she wanted to do. They couldn't deny that their daughter had developed a passion and realized that the best thing they could do was give her some room to explore it.

Her foray into acting, Sara told *Newsday*, was innocent enough. "When I was about seven I went to an opening night party. This agent asked me if I wanted to be in commercials. By the time my mom got up the stairs I had an agent."

Career Girl

As it turned out, Sara did not start in commercials after all, but instead focused on learning more about the craft of acting. Then, when she was nine, Sara landed a role in the 1988 feature film *Rocket Gibraltar*, which starred a very young Macaulay Culkin, legendary actor Burt Lancaster, and a then-unknown Kevin Spacey. Kevin played Sara's father in the critically acclaimed film that launched her career.

In 1990, Sara landed a role as actress Pamela Reed's (*Kindergarten Cop*) daughter on the television series *Grand*. But the sitcom didn't stay on the air for very long, and Sara soon found herself back in what she calls "normal school."

Sara explains, "I went to 'normal school' on and off. Mainly during my teen years I was home-schooled [tutored] because I was working so much." When Sara did *Rocket Gibraltar*, she got her first taste of school on the set. That is, she had a private teacher who taught her the same subjects her friends back in New York were being taught. She says that once she was tutored, she didn't want to go back to the classroom. "I loved being tutored because I got so much attention, and I learned quickly because we would go through book after book and I could go at my own pace."

Sara's time in a conventional classroom was often interrupted by her frequent acting gigs, and yet her parents wanted her to have a "normal" childhood. "I was not allowed to work in the summertime. They made sure that once I did start working I had a relatively normal life."

"Normal" for Sara meant tap-dancing lessons, roller-skating, and skateboarding, collecting bottle caps, and going to sleep-away camp. She learned how to play the guitar and developed a passion for singing and playing folk music. Sara was as normal as she could be. Except for one thing — she wasn't thin like a lot of her classmates. By the time she became a teenager and enrolled in the prestigious Manhattan Professional Children's School, Sara discovered that she was different.

Growing Pains

Sara wrote a first-person essay for *Jump* magazine explaining how being different from the other girls at school began to wear on her self-esteem. "I never thought my body was all that different from those of other girls my age since I was always hanging out with adults, but at school I was the only girl with breasts and hips," Sara wrote. When it was time for Sara to take a mandatory dance class at the school, she admitted that the thought of dancing in a leotard in front of her peers "sickened me."

Discouraged by the competitive nature of her school and fueled by negative feelings of self-worth, Sara began to explore this other side of her personality. "I began playing up the artsy, dark, and mysterious loner type with my black punk-rock clothes, tattoo, and multicolored hair."

Even though Sara's personal interests strayed from the mainstream, her career didn't falter. In 1992, Sara landed a guest spot on the TV sitcom *Roseanne,* which was followed by a role as a series regular in the television show *Phenom* in 1993. Because her career was taking off and she was landing roles that were taped in California, her parents decided it was time the family moved out to Los Angeles. Shuttling back and forth from coast to coast each week, they felt, would be too taxing on the family.

While Sara was excited about her new television series and about making new friends, she was still self-conscious about her size. California is one of the most image-conscious places in the world, and Sara initially felt uncomfortable. The truth, as she eventually discovered, was that she did fit in just the way she was. But it took a couple of years of self-development for Sara to realize this fact.

After beating herself up for being different, Sara learned a valuable lesson. She realized that conforming to be like other people stripped her of her individuality. She learned that people come in different types of packages and that she should embrace what makes her different, not shun it. And she learned all of this while playing her guitar and singing folk songs, which are two of Sara's many talents. Music became therapeutic for her, and the more she played, the better she became. Her talent as a musical performer boosted her self-confidence. Playing guitar is something she still does today.

For the record, Sara says she never once felt pressure from her parents or anyone in Hollywood to lose weight. They all thought she was just perfect the way she was.

Hitting Her Stride

With her confidence back, Sara forged ahead with home-schooling so she could earn her high school diploma early. "I liked it because I'm fast. I didn't have to wait for anybody," Sara enthuses. "If I finished a book in a day I could move on. I graduated when I was sixteen."

After graduation, Sara decided that she

wanted to pursue acting full-time instead of going to college. And within no time she was landing guest roles on television shows like *Ned & Stacey*, *Blossom*, *ER*, *Chicago Hope*, and *The Simple Life*. In 1998 she had a small role in the Jennifer Love Hewitt teen movie hit *Can't Hardly Wait*. Later that same year, the WB was casting a new comedy show titled *Zoe, Duncan, Jack, and Jane*. They tapped Sara for a recurring role as cruel-as-can-be wheelchair-bound student Breeny Kennedy. The show premiered in January 1999 to mixed reviews and average ratings. But it was unanimous that Sara was a standout talent in the cast.

When producers Ryan Murphy and Gina Matthews were looking for just the right person to play Carmen Ferrera on *Popular*, they instantly had Sara in mind. One hitch, though — Sara was already committed to *Zoe, Duncan, Jack, and Jane*. "It certainly was an interesting process," Sara says of being caught in the middle. On one hand, she already had a job. But on the other hand, here was this new show offering her a lead role. Fortunately, everything worked out, much to Sara's delight. "The producers and writers of *Popular* really fought for me."

Sara is having the time of her life on the show and with her fans, who never forget to tell her what a great role model she is. "Earlier in my career I would have been bummed out to play a girl who doesn't make the cheerleading team because she's too heavy, like on *Popular.* But it doesn't [bum me out] anymore," Sara explained in *Jump* magazine. "I don't want to be some sort of poster child for the unpopular, but I hope it will do some good to have a character like Carmen on television."

CHRISTOPHER GORHAM
is Harrison John

Poor Harrison John. All he's wanted all his life is a date with Brooke McQueen, the most popular girl in school. But that will probably never happen, partly at least because he's not, well, popular. Harrison isn't a geek by any means. He's smart, good-looking, athletic, and has a great personality. What Harrison lacks is that little something that the popular guys in school have — physical maturity. Harrison just hasn't caught up with some of the other guys and, right or wrong, that's what attracts Brooke and her friends.

But don't feel sorry for Harrison. He's got great friends in Sam McPherson, Carmen Ferrera, and Lily Esposito. Who needs that beautiful, sweet Brooke Mc-

Queen anyway? If only it were easy to *really* feel that way!

Finding the inspiration to play Harrison isn't difficult for actor Christopher Gorham. "Harrison's banner is that it's important to stay truthful," Chris explains. "He tries to stay honest to himself, but he has a crush on Brooke McQueen that he can't get over. So as a result, he has a big chip on his shoulder about the popular kids."

Star Child

Chris was born and raised in the central California town of Fresno, which is approximately two hundred miles north of Los Angeles. Even though Chris was far from the bright lights of Hollywood, he became interested in entertainment at an early age. Initially Chris's entry into acting was small scale. He started off participating in small church productions when he was a toddler and later was in elementary school plays. His parents, David, a certified public accountant, and Cathryn, a school nurse, immediately recognized that their son was developing a passion.

In the fourth grade, Chris landed a plum role in a school production of *Alice: Through the Looking Glass*. It was a big deal because usually only the sixth graders were given the parts with many lines, while the younger kids were more like extras. But Chris wowed the crowd with his rendition of the Mad Hatter and was awarded best actor by the school!

Although acting certainly was a passion for Chris and he was good at it, his parents weren't able to drop everything so he could pursue it professionally. Nor did he expect them to. A well-rounded kid, he was busy doing lots of other things that interested him, like playing sports. "I was a bit of a jock," Chris says of his childhood. His parents encouraged him to pursue everything that interested him and to be the best student he could be. Chris did just that.

Making a Splash

Most people have trouble finding one thing they enjoy doing. Not Chris. He excelled at school, sports, and acting. Chris jokes that when he was a teen his popularity was on-again, off-again. While he was popular in the eighth grade, that soon changed. "I was a geek again when I was in the ninth grade because I was only four feet eleven inches and everyone else had grown."

But much like his character Harrison John, Chris was able to adapt to the situation. Even though he wasn't as big as some of the other boys in his class, Chris concentrated on doing what he did best — acting, swimming, and his new interest, water polo. By the time he was in high school, Chris reached new heights, literally and figuratively. Not only had he gotten taller, he found himself on the receiving end of two incredible opportunities.

He was accepted to Fresno's Roosevelt School of the Arts, a high school that specializes in developing aspiring performers' skills. At Roosevelt, which was somewhat like the school featured in the old television series *Fame,* Chris was able to learn more about acting and the history of theater among kids with the same showbiz dreams he had.

Of course Chris still had to hit the books pretty hard, but he did manage to find time to continue playing water polo. In fact, Chris was so good at the complicated sport (it's volleyball meets soccer in a swimming pool), his coach selected him and a fellow teammate to attend a summer athletic program at the prestigious Olympic Training Facility in Colorado Springs, Colorado. Traveling to one of the most highly regarded athletic facilities in the world and training with some of the best players and coaches in the world was an amazing experience.

While this was an opportunity of a lifetime and a lot of fun, it was also extremely hard work. This was no summer camp where they roasted hot dogs over an open fire. Chris and his buddy were up early every day and trained for hours in and out of the pool. And they took plenty of notes so that when they returned to Fresno, they could share what they learned with their teammates.

Chris's desire to continue with water polo eventually waned. The long practices left him so physically exhausted, he could barely muster the energy to do his school-work and concentrate on his first love, acting. During high school he worked at Roger Rocka's Dinner Theater. In a sense, these performances were his first forays into professional acting. When he graduated he knew that acting was what he wanted to do. His parents fully supported his decision and asked only one thing in return — that he get a college education.

Los Angeles, Here I Come

Chris enjoyed the academic side of school, so obliging his parents was not a problem. He chose to attend the University of California at Los Angeles (UCLA). Located in Westwood, California, UCLA is not only one of the top universities in the country it also boasts one of the best theater programs in the country. And not so coincidentally, it's located in the entertainment mecca of the world. Chris knew he'd receive an excellent education both in and out of the classroom.

Chris immediately fell in love with the beautiful tree-lined campus, the culturally rich university — and a certain coed named Anel Lopez. Yes, something special happened one day while Chris was in a vaudeville class. The instructor told the students to pair off to perform an acting exercise, and as Chris explained to the *Fresno Bee* newspaper, "I picked her because she was cute."

The exercise called for the students to stand back-to-back and communicate only by asking each other questions. Chris says every time he would ask Anel a question she would respond with "What?" Anel's responses weren't part of the exercise. Because everybody in class was talking so loudly, she couldn't hear what Chris was saying. So he had to repeat practically every question. When they were through with class Chris spoke to her face-to-face and told her flat out he thought he was falling in love with her. Chris was proud of his "little" announcement, but Anel was understandably a little taken aback by the bold statement.

It took several months of seeing each other in class and around campus before they finally went on their first date. And then Anel saw that Chris was a nice guy. The two found that they not only had acting in common but geography, too. When she was a young girl Anel lived in the Fresno area, just miles from where Chris grew up.

After graduating from UCLA, Chris and Anel began pursuing their professional acting careers. And like many other actors, their first jobs in the real world weren't on a stage or in front of a camera. In fact, Chris says he held several odd jobs, including one for a company called Audience Services. This company helps theaters and television shows that film in Los Angeles fill the seats. So every time you hear a television audience laughing in the background of, say, *Friends,* you know that a company like the one Chris worked for helped out in some way!

Role Reversal

It wasn't long after Chris graduated that he started to land some steady acting jobs. Sure, he still earned a paycheck from the Audience Services folks. But his days of working nine to five were numbered once producers and directors in town saw what he could do. Indeed, audiences would soon come to appreciate Chris for his acting skill, not his administrative abilities.

One of his first roles was in the 1997 feature film *A Life Less Ordinary,* which starred Cameron Diaz and Ewan McGregor. Soon after, Chris landed television guest spots on *Spy Game, Saved by the Bell, Buffy the Vampire Slayer, Vengeance*

Unlimited, and *Party of Five.* On *Party of Five,* Chris played Jennifer Love Hewitt's boyfriend for four episodes.

In February 1999, Chris was called in to audition for *Popular.* He says the process of landing the Harrison John role was pretty simple. "I bribed the producers," he quips.

Happily Ever After

Of course Chris *wowed* producers Ryan Murphy and Gina Matthews and landed the role of Harrison right away. But his story doesn't end there. Remember his college sweetheart, Anel? Chris and Anel decided that they were meant to be together forever and got married on January 22, 2000. She now goes by the name Anel Lopez Gorham. Chris says he was bummed that they had to postpone their honeymoon until after the show wrapped up production on its first season.

Fortunately, the newlyweds didn't have to spend too much time apart after their wedding. Ryan and Gina discovered that the talent in the Gorham household wasn't limited to Chris. Anel landed a recurring role as one of Brooke McQueen's fellow Glamazons, Poppy Fresh. These days Chris couldn't be happier. "I'm doing what I like to do, and it's a dream."

TAMARA MELLO
is Lily Esposito

If passion were personified it would be Lily Esposito. She's a young woman with an old soul who has compassion for all creatures — living and dead. Lily believes in goodness, hard work, and standing up for those who can't stand up for themselves.

In the first episode of *Popular*, Lily was confronted with a moral dilemma, one that many high school students face. She had to dissect a frog in biology class. A die-hard vegetarian and animal rights activist, Lily decided to take a stand against the class assignment and just said no to her teacher, Bobbi Glass. Ms. Glass admired Lily's courage but ultimately admonished the behavior and delivered an ultimatum — dissect the frog or receive a failing grade. Lily learned the valuable lesson that some battles are a lost cause no matter how hard they're fought.

Tamara says that she and Lily share similar personality traits. "I think there's parts of me in her and parts of her in me," Tamara explains. "She's more idealistic than I am. She really believes that she can change the world, and I really admire her for that."

In fact, playing the part of Lily inspired Tamara to reflect on her own life. "In doing research for the show I actually became a vegetarian. I learned all this stuff and thought, 'Wow, she's right,'" Tamara says with a giggle. "I've been a vegetarian since we started shooting the show, and it's really been a change for the better in my life."

Tamara jokes that as each episode is filmed, she finds that her character's beliefs continue to influence her in real life. "We did another episode where I tried to save this lobster that was being sold by a restaurant. In real life I was still eating fish. But after that episode I was, like, 'I can't eat that anymore.'" Having sworn off meat, and now sushi and lobster, Tamara jokes, "I'm not going to be able to eat anything by the time the show is finished."

Mello Beginnings

Tamara was born and raised in Orange County, California, and is the oldest of three kids in her family (she has a younger brother and sister). Orange County is where the city of Anaheim is, home to the world-famous Disneyland theme park. John Stamos (*Full House*) and Danielle Fishel (*Boy Meets World*) once lived in that area as kids.

Early on, it was apparent that Tamara was in touch with her feelings and with nature. She was an avid reader, and as a result she learned to express her own thoughts by writing in a journal. Being an actress wasn't much on Tamara's mind when she was a girl. She was more interested in doing well in school and spending time with her friends and family, and Tamara had other career goals: She thought she might want to become an anthropologist.

Unlike her character Lily Esposito, Tamara actually loved school. She was involved to the max, especially with her school's drama club. "I actually started a drama club at my school, and I was in a lot of AP (Advanced Placement) classes, which was hard, but I didn't even think of it at the time," Tamara explains. "I would go to school, then I'd have play rehearsal for four hours, and then I'd go home and stay up doing homework until two in the morning. I pushed myself."

All that dedication paid off as Tamara soon realized her after-school hobby was a passion. She enjoyed reading books and plays, letting her imagination soar, and transforming into different characters on her school's stage. And she was good, too. Unlike other students, who struggled to find their true identity and passion, Tamara knew that theater was for her. It was more fulfilling than anything else she'd ever experienced.

"I tried out for cheerleading my first

year of high school because I thought that was what you were supposed to do. I didn't make it." Tamara shrugs. "And I'm pretty grateful for that because if I had made it, I'm pretty sure I wouldn't have gotten involved in theater."

Despite being heavily involved in theater, Tamara managed to take accelerated courses in high school and earn her diploma at age sixteen. She enrolled in a local college in the fall and declared anthropology as a major. Tamara signed on for a few acting classes to round out her schedule. It turned out to be a wise decision.

"I Wanted to Explore It"

While anthropology was certainly a field that interested Tamara, acting was what she really wanted to do. "I thought acting was fun and interesting and I wanted to explore it," Tamara says simply. Soon after enrolling in acting class, she landed a role in a school play. As fate would have it, someone from the Vanguard Theater Group, a nearby community theater, stopped by Tamara's college to catch the school play. Tamara's performance was good enough to catch the talent scout's eye and land her a role in the Vanguard's production of *To Gillian on Her 37th Birthday*. Tamara officially joined the theater group and landed an agent in no time.

Soon after, the agent booked Tamara a Mountain Dew commercial, and later a guest-starring role on *Boy Meets World*. Legendary television producer Aaron Spelling, who developed hit shows like *The Love Boat* and *Dynasty*, saw Tamara audition for one of his shows, *Beverly Hills 90210*. While she didn't get the part on *90210*, Mr. Spelling was so impressed with her that he offered her a guest-starring role on one of his other shows, *7th Heaven*.

Hollywood producers and casting directors discovered Tamara, and acting roles came more steadily. She had small roles in *The Brady Bunch Movie, Tom and Huck,* and *The Beautician and the Beast* (with Fran Drescher). She was working so frequently, Tamara had to put her college career on hold.

In 1997, Tamara landed a regular role in the television series *Nothing Sacred,* a drama about an unconventional Catholic priest and his parishioners. The show was critically well received but never caught on with the viewing public and was canceled after its first season.

But Tamara wasn't out of work for very long. She performed in a series of feature films including *Rave, Overnight Delivery,* and *Carlo's Wake.* Then in 1999, Tamara found herself smack-dab in the middle of a hit with a role in the Freddie Prinze Jr. film *She's All That.* She also had a small role on the WB's *Zoe, Duncan, Jack, and Jane* before landing the role as Lily in *Popular.*

Tamara's acting career all happened somewhat quickly and naturally. While she enjoys the success her hard work has brought her, acting isn't the be-all and end-all in Tamara's world, which includes her very supportive family, friends, and her twelve-year-old black Pomeranian, Ashby. If she weren't acting, the actress says it's likely she would probably pick up right where she left off and study anthropology.

RON LESTER
is Mike "Sugar Daddy" Bernadino

Everybody should have a friend like Mike "Sugar Daddy" Bernadino. He's kind, loyal, positive-thinking, upbeat, the life of the party. Sugar is popular with the guys on the football team, especially his best friend, Josh Ford. He and Josh roam the Kennedy High halls together like they own the place. They entertain the "in" crowd at their lunch table and always know where to go for the coolest parties in town.

Despite his weight problem — he's obese — Sugar is a chick-magnet. Soon after Texan Mary Cherry moved into town she immediately sidled up to Sugar and accompanied him to Brooke McQueen and Nicole Julian's exclusive A-list bash. With Sugar for arm candy, Mary Cherry became instantly popular. But Sugar isn't your typical life-of-the-party athlete. He's got feelings and emotions, and he's not afraid to show them. In the first season we saw Sugar's tender side when he confessed to Josh that he felt he would be nothing at school if not for his friendship with the school quarterback. Sugar thought that if Josh ditched the football team for the school production of *South Pacific,* he'd lose his social standing at Kennedy High.

Understandably, he's a little envious of Josh, who seems to have everything. Admitting his true feelings was a big step for the big man on campus to take.

But it's precisely those qualities that actor Ron Lester can relate to. Ron will be the first to admit that, like Sugar, he was the big man on campus. He was popular with his classmates and a member of his high school football team. And like Sugar, Ron enjoys socializing and partying and listening to music with friends. But the actor admits he worries about his weight and how it not only affects his social life but his overall health and well-being.

"I'm fat," Ron says. "But it's only part of what I'm about." Similar to Sara Rue's character Carmen Ferrera, Ron hopes that a character like Sugar will help people see that "fat" is not a reason for people to be discriminated against.

Class Clown

Ron was the youngest of four children born to a truck driver and a housewife in Kennesaw, Georgia. Ron will be the first person to tell you that the rural town of Kennesaw, which is located approximately eighty miles from Atlanta, isn't exactly known for its liberal arts background. Kennesaw isn't a place many actors come from. "It's hillbilly country," Ron jokes.

In fact, Ron might be the only actor ever to emerge from Kennesaw. There, many young men go directly from high school to the workforce. When Ron was a young boy he thought he might be a truck driver like his father or perhaps work for one of the large corporations in Georgia, like Lockheed or Coca-Cola. His three siblings, all girls, were much older and had already left home by the time he was in elementary school. He enjoyed learning the skills of outdoor sportsmen, like hunting, fishing, and four-wheel driving. As Ron grew up his parents noticed that their baby had two obvious qualities. For starters, he wasn't a baby — he was one of the biggest kids in school. Second, Ron was extremely outgoing, to the point where teachers felt he was a troublesome student. Truth of the matter, Ron wasn't a bad kid, he was just a ham around his peers. He was bored with schoolwork and much preferred socializing to studying. "I was the kid who was always in the principal's office but could never figure out why," Ron says good-naturedly. "Most kids have one parent-teacher conference during the year. I think I averaged at least three."

He tended to seize appropriate moments in the spotlight at church productions and local theater. "I was in Cobb's Children's Theater in the seventh and eighth grades. I played Mr. Bumble in

Oliver Twist," Ron says proudly. But his acting career didn't last long. "I took drama in high school, and the first week there I mooned the teacher and I got kicked out. That was my drama experience in high school."

Big Man on Campus

With acting on the back burner, Ron focused on football, his favorite sport. Ron was one of the biggest kids in his class and became very muscularly developed at a young age. His large size was a natural for the game, which demands strength, speed, and agility. While attending North Cobb High School he was in excellent physical condition. "I was on the varsity football team when I was a freshman," Ron says proudly. "My sophomore year I was benching 410 pounds. I was always muscular and big. I was a country boy. I was like the ox boy."

While Ron loved football and the other social aspects of school, his grades were really awful. "I was not a good student," Ron admits. "The only A's I got were in art and photography and anything creative." One of his teachers told him that if he didn't shape up and concentrate he'd never amount to anything. The words stunned and upset him because he couldn't quite understand why it was so difficult for him to get decent grades. "I never thought about quitting school," Ron says.

Ron and his parents were baffled. Why was school so hard for him? It was only discovered after Ron graduated from high school that he suffered from dyslexia, a condition that causes people to transpose letters and words on a page and, as a result, have difficulty comprehending material. Ron and his family couldn't believe that the problem had gone undiagnosed for so many years. Once Ron learned what the problem was, he worked on correcting it. Now, he says, "I read one or two scripts a week and these scripts are 140 pages each. I didn't read 140 pages all through high school."

Chapter Two

Ron happily closed the book on the rather unmemorable chapters of high school and began to focus on his future. Not that he had a clue what that future would be. He worked odd jobs for several months until one day when he heard about a commercial that was shooting in town. He decided, on a lark, to try out for it. Initially hired for one day as an extra, Ron's ham-it-up instincts kicked in and he wowed the director. His part expanded into a speaking role. That same acting bug that had bitten Ron when he was a kid playing Mr. Bumble in *Oliver Twist* bit him again! Not to mention the huge payday Ron enjoyed. "I was only supposed to be an extra. I got paid $8,000 for four hours' work. I was twenty and I was hooked."

Ron talked with his mother about wanting to pursue acting as a career. She gave Ron her blessing because she understood that it was the only thing other than football that really captured his attention. She could see the drive in his eyes and feel the passion in his heart. Ron was a man on a mission, and he wasted no time.

With the money from the commercial and some extra funding from his mom, Ron moved to Los Angeles to try to make it. He decided to try his hand at stand-up comedy and soon became a crowd pleaser at popular Los Angeles clubs like The Laugh Factory, The Improv, and The Ice House, where Rosie O'Donnell performed her popular VH-1 series *Stand-Up Spotlight.*

In 1996, Ron met Brian Robbins, a former actor who starred in the 1980s sitcom *Head of the Class.* Brian, now a producer-director for the popular Nickelodeon sketch comedy series *All That,* was working on his first feature film, *Good Burger,* and he invited Ron to audition, something Ron had never done before. Fueled by his "what the heck" attitude, Ron did the best audition he could, and Brian was blown away! He couldn't believe that Ron hadn't acted professionally before. Ron landed the role of Spatch, a crazy hamburger flipper at the fictional fledgling restaurant Good Burger.

"They Call Me 'Gucci Country'"

The movie was a hit and so was Ron. Brian Robbins tapped Ron again to star opposite *Dawson's Creek* star James Van der Beek in the 1999 hit movie *Varsity Blues*. Ron's turn as footballer Billy Bob earned him great reviews and a shot at auditioning for *Popular* and another one-hour show called *Freaks & Geeks*. Ron landed parts on both shows but ultimately committed to play Sugar on *Popular* because it was as a cast regular. Still, Ron filmed several episodes of *Freaks & Geeks* before it was canceled.

All of this fame and success hasn't gone to Ron's head. He's still as down-to-earth as he was growing up in Kennesaw, but Ron has made a few concessions to stardom. He drives a fancy Ford Expedition sport utility vehicle and loves to talk on his cell phone. Ron laughs, "That's where I got my nickname. They call me 'Gucci Country.' You can take the boy out of the country, but you can't take the country out of the boy. For a kid that none of the teachers really bought, I'm doing all right."

LESLIE GROSSMAN
is Mary Cherry

It's often said that there are two kinds of people in the world, those who lead and those who follow. Well, when it comes to Mary Cherry, it's hard to decide which one she is. She's a leader in the sense that she loves to instigate. She'll happily initiate devious activity any chance she gets, especially when it benefits her and makes others look bad. For example, Mary Cherry really wanted to be crowned Kennedy High's homecoming queen and didn't care what she had to do or who she had to hurt to get there. The front-runner was, of course, school sweetheart Brooke McQueen. Mary tried to beat Brooke by spreading rumors and defacing campaign posters. But in the end, her smear tactics backfired, and Brooke went home with the tiara.

As for Mary Cherry being a follower, well, she is a Nicole Julian devotee and will do anything Nicole says. Actress Leslie Grossman says playing Mary Cherry is a hoot. "Mary Cherry is there to be complete and total, one hundred percent, over-the-top comedic relief. And that's just fine by me. I love it and I'm really comfortable in that arena. I adore playing her."

It's important to remember, though, that Leslie is acting. That is, she's nothing like Mary Cherry in real life. "Not even a little bit," Leslie says. "The character is out there. Way out there."

Beach Baby?

Leslie was born and raised in one of the most famous beach towns in America — Santa Monica, California. It's located approximately fifteen miles west of Hollywood, right along the beautiful, rugged California coastline, where bikini-clad beach babes and dudes with surfboards rule. It's where the phrase "endless summer" was coined because the weather is beautiful year-round. Leslie says her older brother (her only sibling) fit right in with that lifestyle. But she didn't. "I was not a surfer girl at all," Leslie says. "I weighed about thirty pounds more than I do now, I had bad skin. That was a little bit isolating in high school."

When Leslie was growing up she found she was more interested in reading and watching television than she was in trying to conform to the social pressures of California. There was a lot of it. Not only did she live in a beach town, but it's also the entertainment capital of the world. She was surrounded by pop cultural images of beauty, and at times she felt very alone. She felt that the best way for her to fit in and make friends was to accentuate the positive — her winning personality. "I figured that if I wasn't going to be popular because I was the pretty girl, I'd better find other things about myself that would make me attractive to people," Leslie explains. "I knew that I was funny, so I figured, 'Be funny and you'll make friends that way.'"

Leslie's social strategy worked! By allowing her witty personality to shine through, she soon expanded her social circle and became more comfortable with being herself. Looking back, Leslie says, "It was a great learning experience. I think I developed parts of my personality that girls who were 'just pretty' didn't."

A Natural

Leslie's innate ability to make others laugh was a gift that she took for granted for many years. Leslie attended Crossroads, a private liberal arts high school in Santa Monica. Many of the students who attend Crossroads are children of professionals in the entertainment industry, and the school nurtures its students' creative endeavors.

Leslie became involved with the theater group at Crossroads but tended to hover in the background because, she says, when it came time to actually perform in front of her peers, she was scared. She was fine when she was acting up at lunch with her friends, but having to go up onstage and act was a frightening prospect. She feared that she'd be judged or ridiculed by her peers. The insecurity was so overwhelming, she decided to become involved in other aspects of theater, such as writing and directing.

Like many of her Crossroads classmates, Leslie went to college. She enrolled in the prestigious Sarah Lawrence College in New York, thousands of miles away from her sunny Southern California home. While she remained involved with theater, Leslie never got up enough courage to perform until her senior year. At the urging of a close friend, Leslie auditioned for a role in a campus production called *Serial*. She landed a lead role, and much to her surprise, she actually liked being onstage! Her confidence rose as she performed each night. By the end of the year, the play had been picked up by an off-Broadway theater in New York City. Leslie, who had never performed before this play, found herself in a position that most actors and actresses only ever dream of. She had to pinch herself to make sure it was all real — and it was!

Leslie found herself on the cusp of something big, and she couldn't have been happier. The only thing she regretted was that she hadn't gotten up the nerve to perform sooner. Rather than think about what she could have done in the past, Leslie knew that she had found her calling. She performed her heart out in *Serial,* which eventually moved out to Los Angeles. Once back in her hometown, Leslie met up with an agent who caught one of her performances. After the play ended, Leslie began auditioning for other jobs. She landed a hosting gig for a British television show called *More American Trash.* The show highlighted clips of bad American television and Leslie had a blast. "I couldn't believe I was getting paid to do acting!"

Nicole? Mary Cherry?

When the producers of *Popular* put out a casting call for the show, they were looking for a very special someone to play nasty Nicole Julian. During the audition process, they found themselves faced with a dilemma of choosing between two actresses for the role — Leslie and Tammy Lynn Michaels. Leslie says she was called back several times to read lines for the producers, and each time she went, there was Tammy Lynn Michaels.

"Tammy and I hit it off, and we started talking at the first audition we ever met at," Leslie says. "We kept getting called back, and we kept seeing each other. First it was with five other girls, then three other girls, then it was down to both of us. At this time, the character Mary Cherry didn't even exist."

Because of the fiercely competitive nature of acting, it's rare that two actresses vying for the same role befriend each other. In fact, it's standard practice not to talk to each other. But Tammy and Leslie clicked early on and decided that no matter what the outcome of their auditions, they would still be friends.

Generally, the last stage before an actor

or actress is offered the role is what's known as a network reading. Basically, the producers present network executives with their top choice or choices for a role. Sometimes there can be thirty or forty people watching the audition. Talk about nerve-racking! Leslie and Tammy each auditioned for the network. Afterward, the producers told them something they'd heard before, "We'll call you." In other words, they walked away not knowing which of them had earned the part.

Well, both their phones rang later that day, but as fans know, Tammy got the role of Nicole. Leslie was bummed when she heard she'd lost. But the person on the other end told Leslie that while she wasn't right for Nicole, they did feel she was excellent for a part they wanted to create just for her — the role of Mary Cherry. Leslie and Tammy had exhibited so much chemistry when they auditioned that the producers felt they had to have both actresses on the show.

Viewers would certainly agree with the producers that Leslie is perfect as Mary

Cherry and Tammy is perfect as Nicole. And in true life-imitates-art fashion, the two actresses have forged a wonderful friendship. What's more, had Leslie landed the Nicole part instead of the Mary Cherry role, she would have missed out on the opportunity to work with actress Delta Burke (*Designing Women*). Delta plays wealthy socialite Cherry Cherry, Mary Cherry's mother. The chemistry between Delta and Leslie is so incredible, you'd think they were actually mother and daughter in real life. "I was so intimidated to work with her," Leslie says. "But she is the most giving, kind woman. Everybody loves her."

Wedding Bells

Leslie was engaged to be married when she landed the *Popular* gig, which kind of put a cramp in her wedding and honey moon plans. She and her husband got married in October 1999 while the show was in production. Like Christopher Gorham and Anel Lopez Gorham, Leslie and her husband had to postpone their honeymoon until after the show wrapped in spring 2000.

Being married hasn't gotten in the way of Leslie's relationships with the single members of the cast. She and some of the others often find time to shop or grab a movie together. "My hobby is being social and spending time with people I love," Leslie says, noting that she feels really lucky that things turned out so well for her. "The show is so creatively satisfying. I adore it. We're also all very close friends. The people who visit our set say, 'You don't know how lucky you are. This is not normal.'"

TAMMY LYNN MICHAELS

is Nicole Julian

Nicole Julian is the one person in school everyone wants to befriend. Not because she's nice. Quite the contrary. She's one of the nastiest people around. She's happiest when others are miserable, and she takes great joy in seeing others fail. For example, when Carmen Ferrera tried out for the cheerleading squad she wowed everyone — except Nicole.

Sure, Nicole admitted, Carmen could perform the cheers and dances as well as anyone else on the squad. But for Nicole, image is everything, and Carmen just didn't fit the mold of a cheerleader because she was fat. So Nicole unfairly eliminated Carmen from the squad's final cut.

So why on earth would anyone want

to hang with the most mean-spirited person on the planet? Simply said, Nicole is popular. She wears great clothes, drives a convertible, knows all of the latest trends, and most of all, she projects an attitude and a self-confidence that say, "Don't mess with me."

Actress Tammy Lynn Michaels loves playing the diva of the school. "Honestly, I don't think she's bad enough," Tammy says of her over-the-top mean TV persona. Seriously, though, Tammy says it's fun to play the bad girl instead of the Goody Two-shoes, although there are times when people who watch the show automatically assume she's going to be as mean in real life as she is on TV. "Right after the show started, when I was first getting recognized, people would just stare at me like they were really scared of me. They would whisper to each other."

Now that the show has been on an entire season, Tammy gets recognized more and more frequently. And people are less shy about approaching her once they see how friendly she is. "A lot of people come up to me. They're still really hesitant," Tammy says, noting that fans are very respectful of her privacy. "A lot of little girls ask their moms to ask me for my autograph. It's really sweet."

Homegrown Talent

When Tammy was a young girl growing up in Lafayette, Indiana, she was anything but a diva-in-training. Lafayette is located in the country's Midwest region, where farming is the major industry. Tammy and her older sister were raised by their single mother, who often worked several jobs at once to make ends meet. It was a challenge for the entire family. Because her mother had to work so much, Tammy was regularly watched by a baby-sitter. The baby-sitter made sure Tammy and the other kids did their homework and stimulated their creative minds. Best of all, she encouraged the kids to sing and dance, finger paint, and just have fun being kids.

Tammy and some friends enjoyed play-acting in the baby-sitter's backyard. They would talk about television shows they liked, assign characters for each other to play, then reenact what they'd seen. It was like they were putting on little television shows of their own. Tammy had a blast performing backyard theater. It was the only place where she really felt she belonged. The other kids understood her in a way that her other friends at school didn't.

"I got involved in any sort of pretending that I could in elementary school," Tammy explains, noting that for years she felt like a misfit with her classmates. "When I got to junior high I realized there was something called the drama club that went along with what I liked doing."

It was a revelation for Tammy to learn that the childhood game she loved was something that other kids played. Her childhood game was actually a legitimate course of study, and Tammy knew she'd found her calling.

Polar Opposite

With the drama club, Tammy had finally found a place where she felt she belonged. It's ironic that Tammy wasn't popular when she was in school. She says she was the polar opposite of her *Popular* character, Nicole Julian. "In the drama department I was popular, but to the rest of the school we were all just a bunch of freaks," Tammy says. "I didn't have many friends."

Tammy told *Jump* magazine, "Eighth grade was my cootie year. No one would talk to me. I was miserable. And I don't blame people for thinking I had cooties, either, 'cause I probably thought I had them myself."

The "in" crowd, meaning the cheerleaders and the jocks, not only didn't care much for Tammy and her drama friends, they were rude in the hallways and lunchroom and pretty much made going to school an unpleasant experience. How ironic that years later Tammy could draw upon her high school past to muster up just the right sass and savvy to play Nicole Julian!

Thankfully, Tammy didn't let those kids or her nonpopular status affect her dreams and goals. She was a good student, a good daughter to her mother, and an excellent actress-in-training. Tammy hung with her drama club pals and soon starred in school productions of *The Wizard of Oz, Hello Dolly,* and *Cyrano de Bergerac.*

Country Girl to City Slicker

After graduating from high school, Tammy moved to New York City to pursue a professional acting career. She knew that making it in the theater capital of the world would be difficult. Armed with enthusiasm, passion, and a little bit of money in her bank account, Tammy was ready to take the city by storm. Because acting is one of the most competitive professions in the world, there are only a few jobs available, and hundreds, sometimes thousands of actors audition for them. So like most struggling actors have done at one time or another, Tammy worked some odd jobs to help pay the rent.

Tammy says that those lean years as a struggling actress were, well, pretty lean. New York City is an expensive place to live, and Tammy did everything she could to survive. "I couldn't afford milk, so I would have dry cereal and water," Tammy explains. She worked as a costumed elf at Macy's department store, a bartender, a baby-sitter, and a waitress. All of the odd jobs she held also helped Tammy afford to take classes to hone her craft. The days and nights were long, and Tammy began to wonder if she would ever get a break. One day, as she'd done many times before, Tammy met with a talent manager. This manager, however, was so taken with Tammy that she signed her on the spot. Soon after, Tammy booked a small role on the hit drama *Law and Order.* Her career had officially begun!

Tammy wasn't ready just yet to give up

all her odd jobs. But she did have to juggle her schedule a bit to accommodate all the acting gigs that came her way. She landed a series of commercials for products like Kentucky Fried Chicken, Secret deodorant, and Sprint. With the steady good pay that the commercials provided, Tammy could afford milk and any other groceries she wanted without worry. What a concept — cereal with milk!

Coast to Coast

With steady commercial work streaming in, it was suggested to Tammy that she try to take her career to the next level. Every year in Los Angeles, the television production studios have what's called pilot season. That's when writers and producers present new television series ideas to the networks. Tammy had never been to Los Angeles in her life, and she wasn't sure she wanted to go, either. But she decided it couldn't hurt to at least give it a try. After all, the commercials were fun, but she did have more to offer the viewing public than just thirty or sixty seconds' worth of material.

She flew to Los Angeles, and within the same week auditioned and eventually landed the role of Nicole Julian. Even though her television alter ego vastly differs from her own personality, Tammy says she couldn't feel more at home when the cameras are rolling.

"I love being Nicole, and I love the people I work with," Tammy gushes. And to think she had reservations about taking that fateful trip to Los Angeles.

Call it fate, call it karma, but everything seems to have fallen into place for Tammy. And as for those nasty kids in high school who made fun of her, the actress feels their behavior only made her a stronger individual. "My life has been great. Everything that has happened has taught me something, and I wouldn't change anything. If the tiniest thing had been different, then I wouldn't be where I am now."

BEHIND THE SCENES
AT *POPULAR*

The important thing to remember when watching *Popular* is that it's just a television show. It's fiction, not reality. And nothing proves that more than a visit to the *Popular* set. It's part of the charm of the show for the characters to scoff at and despise one another. But when the cameras aren't rolling, this kooky cast couldn't be closer.

Actress Sara Rue (Carmen Ferrera) says the closeness of the cast and crew is something she's come to treasure. "It's rare that you work with people you hang out with on the weekends," Sara says. "Like, when you're having a party, they're the first people you think to invite. That makes it extra nice."

Ron Lester (Sugar Daddy) agrees wholeheartedly with Sara. "It's a big family," he says proudly. Because the actors work such long hours on the set each week, it's a blessing that they all get along so well. Ron says, "We stay together through the fifteen-sixteen-hour days."

The Place to Be

Kennedy High School and its students actually exist on two soundstages on the Disney Studios lot in Burbank, California, where mega-successful shows like *Home Improvement* and *Boy Meets World* used to tape. Like many television studios, the Disney lot is a massive expanse of land surrounded by fences and security guards. Inside the gated area are more than a dozen soundstages, big warehouselike structures that contain the sets or backdrops for the shows. Because most of the scenes in *Popular* take place either at Brooke and Sam's house or at Kennedy High, there are two soundstages (one for each) devoted to the show.

Inside the Kennedy High School soundstage, one can roam the locker-filled hallways, eat lunch at the cafeteria, or perform an experiment in the biology lab. The other soundstage contains the interior of Brooke and Sam's house, including the two-sink bathroom, the kitchen, and the dining room.

The Brooke-Sam house set also has something of interest to the rest of the cast and crew — the craft services room, where the cast and crew can pick up a snack, a soda, or lunch. It's the most popular place on the set, a minikitchen with a fridge, a toaster, a microwave, and enough food to satisfy any hunger craving. This is where Bryce and Christopher usually grab a banana or an apple to munch on in between scenes.

How It All Works

Popular is a show that has a large core of actors and an even larger extended group of extras to work with each week. Many one-hour dramas feature a cast of four to eight regulars. But on *Popular,* there are nine full-time actors. And not only are those nine actors on the set almost every day, but several recurring characters (Brooke's dad and Sam's mom, both teachers), dozens of extras (actors who fill up the Kennedy High hallways and lunchrooms), and the behind-the-scenes crew show up each day. That many people on the set each day sounds chaotic, doesn't it? Luckily, things don't get out of hand, thanks to *Popular*'s talented crew, which is led by an extremely organized production coordinator who keeps the show on schedule each day.

As Ron mentioned, the workdays can sometimes run as long as sixteen hours. Anybody who watches *Popular* knows that it takes time to get Glamazon-ready! That's one place where fiction crosses over into reality. It takes so long to put the show together each day because all of the girls need to get their hair and makeup done. Ron, Christopher, and Bryce can breeze in and out of the makeup and wardrobe trailer in no time flat. But Carly, Tammy

Lynn, Tamara, Sara, and both Leslies have to allow enough time for hair and makeup before they begin shooting their scenes. Because there are so many actors to prep, the daily routine often begins as early as 5:30 A.M. each day, just as the first pot of coffee is being brewed.

Says Leslie Grossman, "I love working on the show. But the only thing I wish I could change is the hours. Our hours are not normal. We shoot for nine months, and it's nine months of jet lag. You start your call time Monday morning at five-thirty, and by the time Friday rolls around, you're not getting into work until six at night and getting home at five in the morning. It's a real challenge. But unfortunately, that's the way these shows have to be filmed."

While the cast is getting ready and being informed of last-minute script changes, lighting and sound crews prepare the sets for the day's upcoming scenes. It's important that microphones and lights are positioned in the right places so that the actors can be seen and heard when they're taping their scenes. Because this is such a long and at times tedious process, each actor has what's known as a "stand-in" or a "double." A stand-in is a person who physically resembles the actor. For example, say Carly and Leslie Bibb have a scene in their bathroom at home. Rather than have the actresses stand in place for an hour while the crew adjusts the lights and camera angles, the doubles enter the bathroom and stand in (get it?). If it weren't for stand-ins, the actors wouldn't have enough energy to do their scenes. Naturally, scenes that involve more actors require more time and energy to prep. That's why it sometimes takes seven or eight days to shoot a one-hour episode.

Downtime

Because of the lengthy process of putting the show together, the actors have a lot of time in between scenes. But it's generally not enough time to go home or run to the mall or grab a bite to eat at Mc-

Donald's. So what do the actors do when they're not working?

Chances are they can be found inside their trailers — mobile homes on the lot where the actors can rehearse and rest in between scenes. Each trailer has a couch, a vanity makeup counter and mirror, a refrigerator, a television-VCR unit, and a bathroom.

Everyone tries to grab a nap when possible. Leslie Bibb and Tammy Lynn often catch up with friends and family on their respective cell phones, while Christopher tends to mellow out with a good book or hang out with his wife, Anel.

Fast Friends

None of the cast knew one another before they started working on the show. But within weeks, they all became fast friends. Ron and Bryce instantly paired up as best buds, as did Tammy Lynn and Leslie Grossman and Tamara and Sara. Even though there's a seven-year age difference between Leslie Bibb and Carly, the two get along fabulously (unlike their characters) and often participate in interviews and photo shoots together. Leslie B. and Carly attended Nickelodeon's *13th Annual Kids' Choice Awards* together, where they presented an award. (Maybe they'll be nominated next year.) Backstage at the awards show, Leslie B. gushed to the press about her friendship with Carly. "We didn't even know each other before we did the show, and now we're like sisters."

Carly echoes Leslie B.'s sentiments, saying that whenever anyone wants company, whether it's for a quick chat or a stroll down to the Disney commissary, "It's just a matter of going to someone's trailer and knocking on the door."

This kind of open-door policy works for Tamara, who often brings her black Pomeranian, Ashby, to the set with her. Known for his affectionate personality, fluffy little Ashby has become somewhat popular himself. Leslie Grossman confesses, "He is the sweetest dog. Sometimes

I pretend he's mine, and I bring him to my trailer."

Speaking of trailer hopping, Ron enjoys taking turns hanging out in Bryce's trailer or in his own, which he has dubbed "The Sugar Shack." "I have little disco balls hanging from the ceiling. When I'm just hanging out, we play some Sony Playstation, listen to music." Much like his character, Sugar Daddy, Ron is one of the friendliest guys on *Popular*'s campus. Even on his days off Ron likes to visit the set to see what everyone else is up to. Wherever Ron goes, laughter is sure to be heard. He's the comic relief of the bunch, always ready to tell a story and eager to listen to others' tales.

"Bryce is one of my best friends," Ron says proudly.

And Bryce feels the same way about Ron. "I come here every day with a smile on my face. The cast members are just awesome. Every one of them is so cool and talented."

When Bryce has some free time, he enjoys reading, sleeping, working on a screenplay, or playing a game of pickup football or basketball (there's a hoop on the lot) with Chris, Ron, and members of the crew.

Pals Sara and Tamara say they feel very lucky to know each another. They share an adjoining trailer. That is, their trailers have separate entrances and separate spaces but are joined in the middle by a common wall. Says Tamara, "We got really lucky being right next to each other here, and we've gotten really close. We see each other all the time outside of work."

In their free time, Sara and Tamara enjoy reading and talking. Sara sometimes brings her acoustic guitar to work so she can practice playing. She and Tamara collaborate on their scenes and, more important, experiment with various snack creations. "We made this one snack by putting a yogurt pretzel in between two deli potato chips," Sara giggles. "It's the perfect combination of salt and sweet! It's really good."

They may be convincing foes on screen, but Leslie G. says she and the *Pop-*

ular gang have made a true connection off camera. "We see each other all the time, and they're now a part of my regular friends. We all go out together a lot. My hobby is being social and spending time with people I love."

WHO'S POPULAR?

Okay, there's no denying these guys are *all* popular now. They grace the pages of teen and fashion magazines, they attend movie premieres and awards shows, they wear the latest fashions. But what about when they were in high school? Here's what the gang has to say about their school days.

Leslie Bibb

"I went to an all-girls' Catholic high school where there were thirty-eight girls in my graduating class. So it's a little bit different from most high schools. But yet I don't know a high school anywhere in the United States or in the world where popularity doesn't reign over everyone. In junior high I was a cheerleader, but mostly because my sisters were. When I got to high school I was, like, 'I hate cheerleading.' It just wasn't cool anymore to me. So I played tennis, I volunteered a lot. I spent as much time being popular as I did unpopular."

Carly Pope

"My high school didn't have such a strict social order. It was more mingled and meshed. There wasn't this division because of the jocks and the alternative kids, like on the show. In Vancouver we didn't have cheerleaders, so I'm very foreign to that concept. But there definitely was division within the groups, it just wasn't stereotypical. It was just everybody in his or her own group and they chose to hang out with the people they wanted to hang out with. But they were welcomed into the other groups. You know, there was *opportunity* for crossover, but that didn't necessarily happen all the time. I was very involved in sports in school. I loved just about every-thing — basketball, volleyball, soccer, ten-nis, snowboarding."

Bryce Johnson

"The cliques on the show are very sim-ilar to the kinds of cliques that existed in my high school. I had a great time all the way through high school. I guess you could say I was popular. I loved extracurricular activities in school because there was noth-ing much to do when I just went home. I got involved in soccer and golf and a little bit of baseball and basketball. I did student council. I was really active in school, and I tried to do as much as I could. I didn't care much for schoolwork, but I had fun else-where."

Sara Rue

"It's hard for me to say since I went to 'normal' school on and off. We didn't have cheerleaders in New York, so I never really dealt with that in school. I had good friends. There weren't cliques in my school like there are on the show."

Tammy Lynn Michaels

"I was very, very unpopular in high school. There was a group of kids — the cheerleaders and the jocks — and they hated me and my friends. By the time I got to high school, in my junior year, there was a bunch of us drama geeks who banded together and we'd stay up late at night and we just kind of carried each other through high school."

Christopher Gorham

"I think the show is a fairly accurate [depiction] of how school really is. When I was in school, kids were really brutal to one another. I think a great part of our show is that if one of the characters has a beef with another character, he or she is going to confront it. They're not going to waffle around the subject, which is what I saw a lot in high school. Throughout junior high and high school I really flip-flopped back and forth as to whether I was accepted or not. . . . You know, in eighth grade I was popular, ninth grade, suddenly I was a geek again."

Ron Lester

"I think I was probably popular. I played football, had a good time."

ROLL CALL

LESLIE BIBB'S BEAT

Birth Date: November 17, 1974

Born In: Bismarck, North Dakota

Raised In: Nelson County, Virginia, and Richmond, Virginia

Siblings: Has three older sisters, Tricia, Kim, and Bev

Pets: Jack, an Australian shepherd-Rottweiler mix. His nickname is Count Blackula.

Education: Graduated from St. Gertrude's High School in Richmond, Virginia; attended the University of

Virginia for one semester before moving to New York City to pursue a modeling and acting career

Acting Idols: Jessica Lange and Al Pacino

Fave Movies: *Waiting for Guffman* and *When Harry Met Sally*

Musical Tastes: Gus Gus, Jude, the *Magnolia* sound track

Snacks On: Wheat Thins

Hobbies: Enjoys volunteering, hiking, hanging out with her friends

Little-known Fact: "I'm a really spazzy, geeky person. I think people think I'm much cooler than I really am."

Upcoming Movie: Leslie stars next in the comedy, *See Spot Run,* with David Arquette

CARLY'S CORNER

Birth Date: August 28, 1980

Born In: Vancouver, British Columbia, Canada

Raised In: Vancouver

Siblings: Two brothers, Kris (older) and Alex (younger)

Education: Attended a bilingual French-English school from kindergarten until seventh grade; graduated from Lord Byng High School in 1998; attended University of British Columbia for one semester before landing the role on *Popular* and moving to Los Angeles

Musical Tastes: Everything from reggae to electronica

Favorite School Subjects: Foreign languages and math

Fave Movie: *Labyrinth*

Fave Book: *Jitterbug Perfume* by Tom Robbins

Favorite Food: Japanese

Role Model: "I admire anyone who takes pride in what they do."

Hobbies: Carly is a sports fanatic — she loves to play basketball, baseball, and volleyball, and swim.

First Big Break: Carly was discovered by an agent while she was performing in an all-female *Odd Couple!*

Upcoming Movie: Look for Carly in *The Glass House,* with Leelee Sobieski

THE BUZZ ON BRYCE

Birth Date: April 18, 1977

Born In: Reno, Nevada

Raised In: Denver, Colorado, and Sioux City, Iowa

Siblings: Two brothers, Brendon (older) and Brett (younger)

Education: Graduated from high school in 1995; attended Western Iowa Tech for one semester before moving to Los Angeles to study acting at the American Academy of Dramatic Arts

Best Thing About Acting: "Being able to work in front of an audience of millions of viewers and getting paid to do it."

Favorite Things to Do When Not Acting: Golf, beach volleyball, football

Fave TV Show: *The Simpsons* and VH-1's *Behind the Music* series

Fave Movie: *Ghostbusters*

Currently Reading: *Conversations with God*

Musical Tastes: Everything and anything — Elvis, Frank Sinatra, R&B, and oldies

Favorite Food: Italian

Hobbies: Bryce is a movie fanatic. He tries to see everything!

Favorite Holiday: Christmas. "It's a good time to get together with your family, and there's presents and good food."

SARA'S STATS

Birth Date: January 26, 1979

Born In: New York, New York

Raised In: New York, New York, and Los Angeles, California

Siblings: One sister, younger

Pets: Three cats, Miss Phipps, The Kraken, Orange Popsicle "Pop" Number 5; Bearded dragon, Norman (like an iguana only smaller)

Education: Earned high school diploma in 1995 (she was tutored and graduated at age sixteen)

Fave TV Show: *Will & Grace*

Current Fave Movies: *Magnolia* and *The Cider House Rules*

Musical Tastes: Loves Bob Dylan and Ani DiFranco

Favorite Food: Sushi

Favorite School Subjects: English and math

Little-known Fact: Sara is an avid animal enthusiast and as such is a vegetarian.

Hobbies: Enjoys reading, playing the guitar, and singing

TAMMY LYNN'S TIDBITS

Birth Date: November 26

Born In: Lafayette, Indiana

Raised In: Lafayette, Indiana

Siblings: An older sister

Education: Graduated from high school

Fave Actress: "I'm obsessed with Rosemary Clooney" (George's aunt)

Fave TV Show: *Will & Grace, Northern Exposure* (reruns), *The X-Files*

Fave Movie of All Time: *White Christmas*

Musical Tastes: Simon & Garfunkel, Aerosmith, Guns & Roses

Favorite Snack: Sweetarts

Hobbies: Hiking, writing in her journal, painting

Random Quote: "I don't think that you grow until you graduate from high school."

TAMARA TRIVIA

Birth Date: February 22

Born In: Orange County, California

Raised In: Orange County, California

Siblings: Two, a younger brother and a younger sister

Pets: Dog, a Pomeranian named Ashby

Education: Graduated from high school in 1993; briefly attended college before acting career took off

Acting Idol: Marlon Brando

Fave Movies: *Breakfast at Tiffany's* and *Moonstruck*

Fave School Subject: English

If Not an Actress: "I would probably be an anthropologist."

Musical Tastes: Billie Holiday, Red Hot Chili Peppers, Nirvana

Favorite Food: New York City pizza

Hobbies: Knitting, hiking, yoga

Advice: "Only become an actor if it's the only thing in the entire world that you are passionate about and want to do. It's a really hard profession. It's really hard on your self-esteem. If you just want to do it to be famous or to make money, then it's not worth it."

CHRISTOPHER'S QUICK TAKES

Birth Date: August 14, 1974

Born In: Fresno, California

Raised In: Fresno, California

Pets: Two dogs, a golden retriever named Cuba and a terrier mix named Fred

Education: Graduated from Roosevelt High School of the Arts in 1993; earned bachelor's degree in Film and Theater Arts from UCLA in 1997

Fave Actor: Michael Keaton

Fave TV Show: *Sex & the City*

Fave Current Movie: *Boys Don't Cry*

Fave Books: The Harry Potter series

Musical Tastes: Macy Gray, Ani DiFranco

Favorite Food: Sea bass

Favorite Snack: Pirate's Booty (a low-calorie puffed rice treat)

Hobbies: Enjoys golfing, swimming, learning to speak Spanish

THE RUNDOWN ON RON

Birth Date: August 4, 1975

Born In: Kennesaw, Georgia

Raised In: Kennesaw, Georgia

Siblings: Three older sisters

Education: Graduated from high school in 1996

Fave TV Show: *Freaks & Geeks, The Sopranos*

Favorite Book: The Holy Bible. "It's cool. It points out everything I'm doing wrong."

Fave Movie: *Bladerunner*

Musical Tastes: Loves country & western

Hobbies: Fishing, going to movies, collecting die-cast metal cars

FAN-tastic: Ron loves it when people respond to *Popular,* and to show his appreciation, he tries to answer all of his fan mail.

First big break: Ron was discovered when he was an extra in a Formula 409 commercial.

THE LINE ON LESLIE GROSSMAN

Birth Date: October 25

Born In: Santa Monica, California

Raised In: Santa Monica, California

Siblings: One, an older brother

Education: Graduated from Santa Monica High School; graduated from Sarah Lawrence College in New York

Fave TV Show: *Will & Grace*

Fave Current Movie: *Erin Brockovich*

Fave Books: *Bridget Jones's Diary* by Helen Fielding and *On Spec* by Richard Rushfield

Musical Tastes: Macy Gray, Mary J. Blige

Favorite Food: Barbecued potato chips

Hobbies: Reading, socializing, shopping

If Not for Acting: "I would probably be a shrink. Psychology is something I've always been fascinated with."

WEB SITES AND ADDRESSES

These popular actors and actresses have quite a fan following in teen magazines and on the Internet. For the latest on Nicole, Brooke, Sam, and Carmen, actor bios, and links to other WB programs, log onto *Popular*'s official site, **www.thewb.com**

Or go to **http://tvplex.go.com/touchstone/popular/index2.html** And if you want to express yourself via snail mail, feel free to write to any of *Popular*'s producers or cast at the following address:

POPULAR
Warner Bros. Television Network
4000 Warner Boulevard
Burbank, CA 91522